WINTER JOURNEY

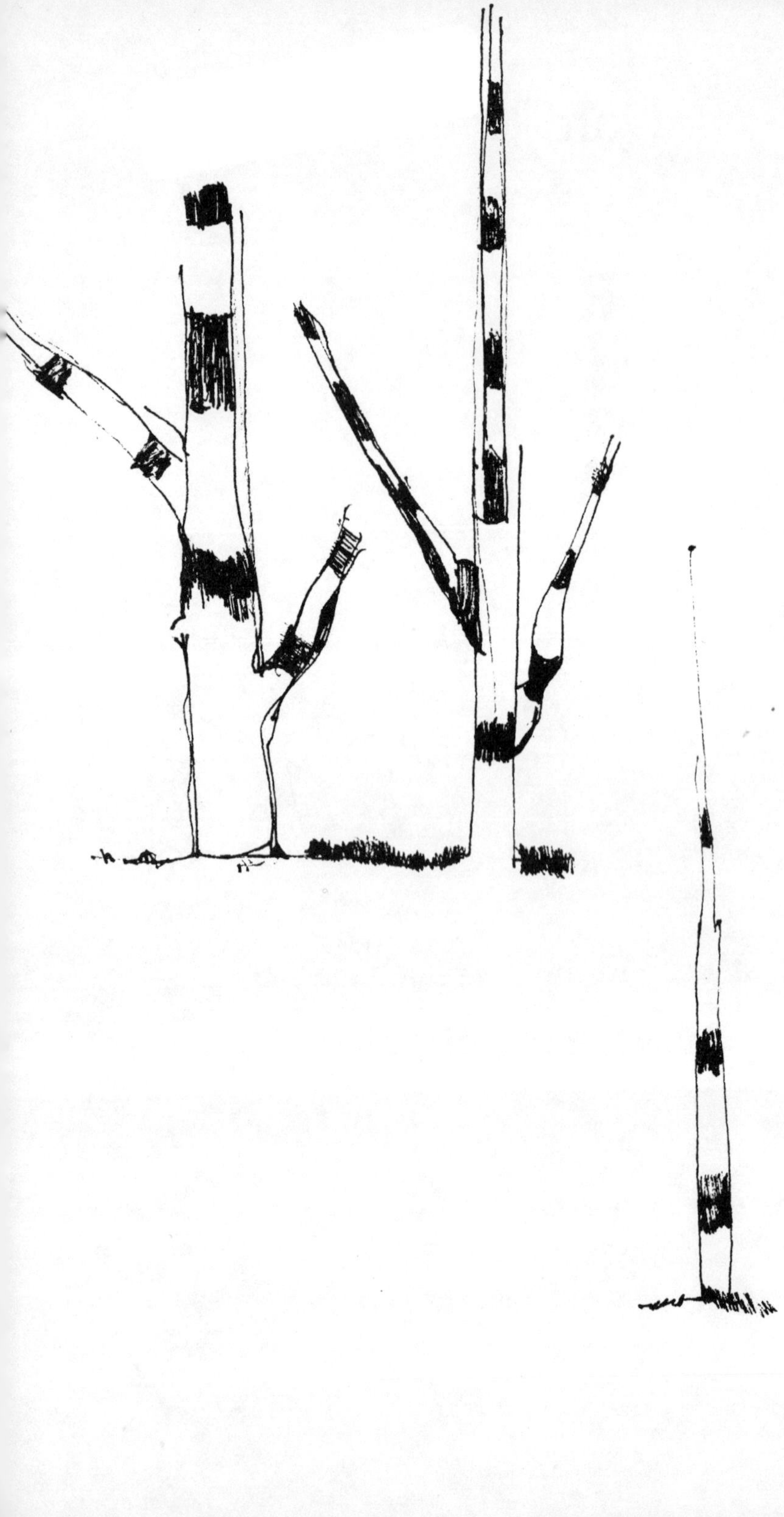

Halvard Johnson

WINTER JOURNEY

with drawings by Basil King

New Rivers Press 1979

Copyright © 1979 by Halvard Johnson and Basil King
Library of Congress Catalog Card Number: 78-68644
ISBN 0-89823-001-2
All rights reserved
Book Design by C.W. Truesdale
Typesetting by Michael Labriole

ALSO BY HALVARD JOHNSON

TRANSPARENCIES & PROJECTIONS (New Rivers)
THE DANCE OF THE RED SWAN (New Rivers)
ECLIPSE (New Rivers)

Acknowledgements: Some of these poems have appeared in the following periodicals—

Dacotah Territory, Northeast, Poetry Now, Juice, Threshings, The Sole Proprietor, Eureka Review, Ironwood, Hanging Loose, Images, Pigiron, and *San Marcos Review.*

This book has been published with the aid of grants from the National Endowment for the Arts and the New York State Council on the Arts.

WINTER JOURNEY was manufactured in the United States of America for New Rivers Press (C.W. Truesdale, editor/publisher), 1602 Selby Avenue, St. Paul, Minnesota 55104 in a first edition of 750 copies of which 15 have been signed and numbered by Halvard Johnson and Basil King.

for Barbie

WINTER JOURNEY

I

11   Variations On A Russian Winter
14   The Silences
15   Blind Cows
16   Killing An Animal In The Rain
17   Poem For The New Year
18   Odin's Wood
20   The Swimmers
21   Lady In Blue
22   Deathfall
23   Fountainebleau: Feeding The Carp
24   First Love
25   Prairie Junction
26   Wild Horses
27   Modus Vivendi
28   Neighborly
29   Intimate Voices
30   Litany

II

33   Barn
34   Moira
35   Stamping
36   Oil
37   Lights
38   Snow
39   Mountain

III

43   A Bad Day
45   Beginning Again
46   Walking You Home
47   Departures
48   Ostinato
49   Nights On Rainy Lake

50 December Morning
51 Refusals
52 Etudes
54 Erosion
55 Dawning
56 My Life In The Revolution
57 Pressure Points
58 Down The Road
59 Nightride
60 Converging Lines
61 Nearing The Moon
62 A Winter's Sun
63 Fault
64 Waiting Room
65 Brain Damage
66 Stunt
67 Disappearing Into The Night
69 Bete Noire
70 Eagle Cove
71 Track South
72 Pavilions

IV

77 Improvisations

V

87 Edge Of The Forest
89 The Incalculable Perfection Of Heaven
90 Paradise Road
91 Salt Spray
92 The Sea And Sinbad's Ship
93 A Little Stream
94 Six Crossings
96 Nova
97 Lyric Suite
99 Winter Journey

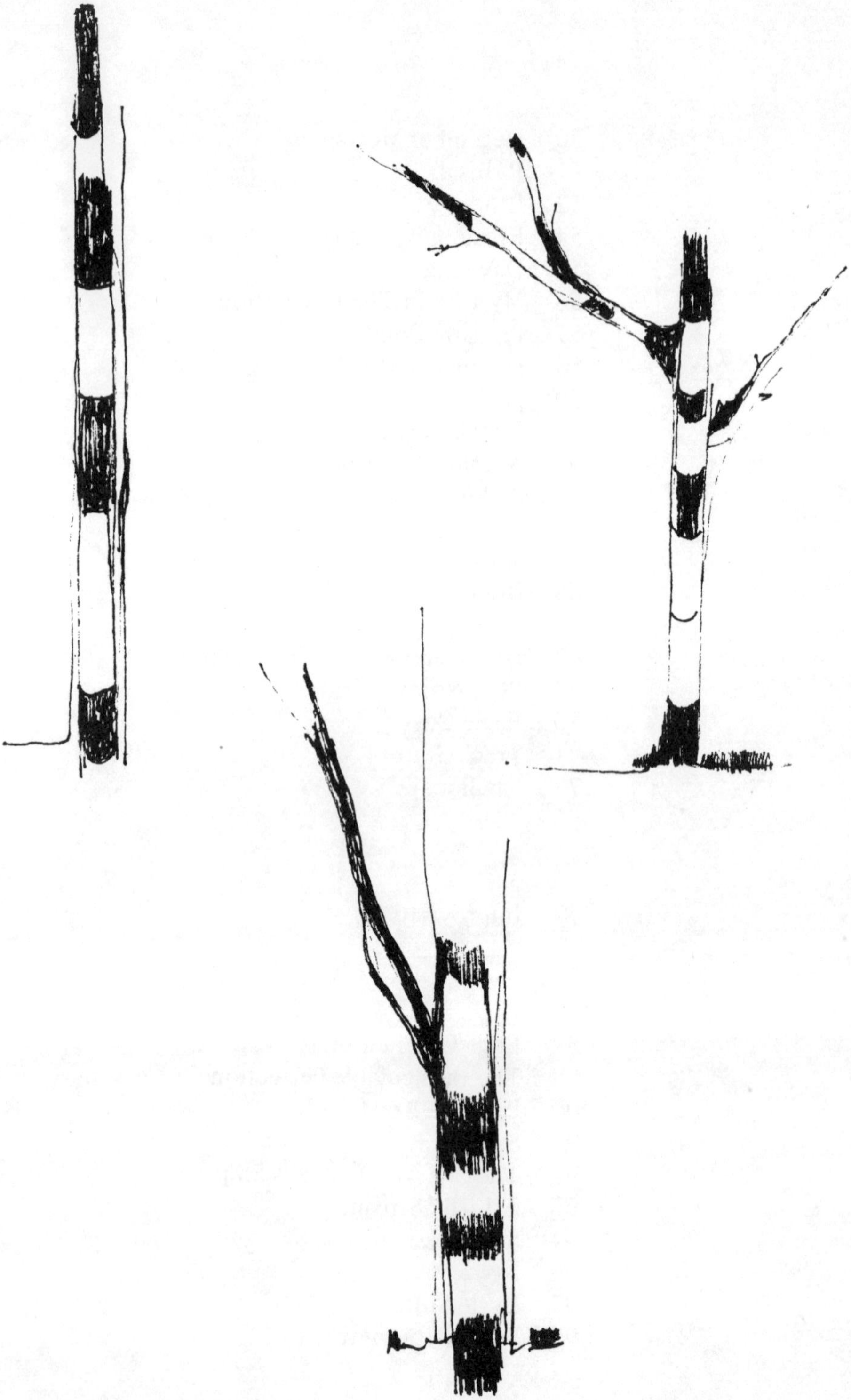

I

VARIATIONS ON A RUSSIAN WINTER

1.

Coming back
we find that our footsteps
are lost in the snow.
We pause at the edge
of a frozen, snow-covered lake,
watch smoke rise from our cabin
where it lies hidden in the trees.
Someone is there now, though we
have been gone for days.
We enter by way of the only door
and find ourselves going about
our daily business—the work,
the small tasks—as though
we had never left.

2.

I have received a letter
and stand outside reading it
in the clear air. The letter is from
a friend in a distant city, and I read it
as though I have not heard from him
in years. But in fact he has been here
quite recently, moving from the dark trees
to the lakeshore and back again. In truth
he is here now, standing at the end
of the ice-bound dock, looking out
across the lake. The letter is
from someone else. Someone I don't know.

3.

Day after day
passes from black to gray to white
and back again to gray and black.
This dullness of everyday living
moves me to despair. The sharp cold
is painful to my senses, but the weather
refuses to be used to relieve my boredom.
Day after dismal day, it is the same—
our tedious conversations always becoming
plumes of breath in the ragged air.

4.

I received a letter
and stood outside reading it
in the clear, dry air. The letter
was from a friend in a distant city,
and I read it eagerly, not having heard
from him for many years. He wrote of events
in the city—bloodshed and turmoil. I stepped
out of the trees and moved toward the lake.
At the end of our dock I paused and looked out
across the frozen lake. His letter was from a world
I didn't know. I returned through the trees to our cabin.

5.

If I look at you from a certain angle
I can almost believe that I have never
seen you before. Once, this was a matter
of hiding among the trees and waiting until
you came along the path. I watched you pause
at the place where normally I would have joined you.
I could see that you were waiting for me,
expecting me, but still I made no move to join you.
And then you went on, hoping to find me already at the lake.

6.

He comes out here from the city
to nurse his wounds and rest. He,
for the moment, is the exiled leader,
and his visits to us are punctuated by those
of others, who come out from the city with news of recent events
or need for instructions. He listens to their concerns
and airily dismisses them. If he is worried or troubled
he shows no signs of it. With us, he drinks and laughs,
making lighthearted jokes about life in the country.

7.

The lake below us wears a skin
of ice. Roads disappear in the hills.
White lost in white today. Cold as the breath of a ghost.
The distant cities with their high buildings and towers
are cold. The smalltown huts of the poor are cold.
No fire, anywhere. A man lies dying in the road.
My breath freezes in his beard. His last words are,
"I have never been so cold." His fingers are so stiff
I have to break them to escape his grip.

THE SILENCES

You call for silence, but I
have abolished that. There is no
place in this world where you
will not hear me whispering
in the next room, or calling to you
from across the street.

I assail you with a constant
stream of words. I talk about
myself—my normal upbringing,
my fears, my hopes. I talk
about you—how you look,
what you have come to mean to me.

Sometimes I read to you. I read you
John Ashbery's poem called "How
Much Longer Will I Be Able to Inhabit
the Divine Sepulcher." I read it
again and again. I read it
to you backwards.

There are tiny moments between words,
between syllables sometimes. You listen to those
and call them silence. But listen closely.
That silence is one of my most subtle voices.
Now you are laughing.
Darkness interrupts my story.

BLIND COWS

Hurrying forward
he perceived a dark,
heavy figure struggling
in the water.
Beast or human, he couldn't say.
Disgust overwhelmed him.
Something in the darkness
was going under.

They don't even have eyes here,
he thought. The surface of the planet
ebbed and flowed. Nothing familiar.
Red blotches on the back of his hand.

In some part of the meadowland
are wanderers, moving among the blind cows.
He—let me say I—I move
with them, cautiously, one step at a
time.

KILLING AN ANIMAL IN THE RAIN

Just a blur, a solid thump,
and I know I have killed it.
I drive on. Barbie's asleep,
doesn't even stir. But what
was it—a cat? a fox?
Long blur, down low in the headlights,
close to the pavement, moving fast.
But not fast (or slow) enough.
Going where? Why such a hurry?
I slow down slightly in shock.
It's dead. It has to be.
Couldn't have lived, and I can't stop.
Not on a road like this. Wet, slick.
Winding through German countryside,
small locked-up towns. It couldn't
have felt a thing. I shrug and
continue—suicide run of my own.

POEM FOR THE NEW YEAR

This is the year
I take you by the throat.
The room in which you hide—
that jerry-built box
of wood and plaster—
crumbles around you.
One smash of my fist
and there is only a gray sky
above you. The words and ideas
you have spun like a cocoon
about you—these I dispel
with a breath. You say
you are only human.
I say you are more than that,
more than a word, a breath.

ODIN'S WOOD

> "I know that I hung on the windy tree
> For nine whole nights,
> Wounded with the spear, dedicated to Odin,
> Myself to myself."
>
> from the *Havamal*

1.

Fingers of wind
wound in my hair.
The fingers were mine
as much as the hair. The wind
hears my voice and obeys.

The wind is my voice and I
am obedient to myself. I hang
and bleed upon my own tree. The tree
is mine and I am both the tree
and he who is hung from the tree.

2.

You, my cloud, take the form of a man
and walk into the village. Ask there whose voice it is
that is heard in the forest when wind wails
mournfully in the trees.

They'll give one of my names. They'll say hereabouts it is Odin's,
the father of poetry, the prophet, the magician.
The great god of wisdom and war.

3.

"Who made the spear?" I'll ask them.
And they will say, "Odin fashioned it."

"And to what end did he make it?"
"To kill himself," they'll say.

"Can the spear kill its maker?" I'll ask.
"In a manner of speaking," they'll say.

4.

On the last night, the moon was low in the sky
when the ravens returned. The intrigues of the court
were whispered in my ear, the secrets of the world. My blood

flowed down my groin, along my legs and feet. It darkened the bark
of the gallows tree and flowed down into the earth,
where it was sucked up by roots, eaten by ravenous worms.

From worms and roots my godhood seeps into bush and tree,
into dove and pheasant and owl and fox and deer and man,
and gods eat men, now don't they? And that way eat themselves.

THE SWIMMERS

They stride briskly along the rocky shore.
The sea is running the other way.
At a twisted piece of driftwood
called "The Agony of an Animal"
they briefly pause to congratulate each other.
They walk on a few steps. Then they stop.
They strip off their clothes and dive into the water.
Now they are nearing the bottom.

LADY IN BLUE

Touched, though essentially
unimpressed, she glides
through our landscape
with all the cool breathiness
of a flute. Her eyes
are like a smoky haze.

Our country here, its gnarled
trees and gunmetal skies,
was hers once too. But she,
returning, brought us
something foreign,
an Italianate grace. A turn
of elegance, where all
that rules is rigid.

Here, where our words
are coined and bitten
off like hard metal, where nothing
exists simply for itself,
she is a gratuitous performance.
A breath enclosed in a platinum
tube. Inconsequentiality,
her extravagent name.

DEATHFALL

A range of wood-drift,
scattered leaves in a thicket,
the girl at one end of a rope.

The marshalling of abilities
is only the first step. Step one, that is,
in the universal parade. She overwhelmed us.
Her ability to do so was never even questioned.

Spider-glass. While out of range
a fleet of trawlers scanned our coastline.
A web of radio signals alerted us
to our most immediate danger.

She walked directly to the podium
and spoke clearly and without hesitation
for several minutes. We knew then
that her beauty had almost deceived us.

    ◊ ◊

Algeria. What was it?
Something about sunshine. The light.
A voice that exploded in the stations of the Paris Metro.

The baroque concerto, its life and times.
The drift of Italy into perpetual chaos and anarchy.
Nervous disorders. There is a twitch in our left eye
which will not leave us.

    And I haven't even mentioned the refusal
    of merits, the frozen North, the daily wastes,
    fiberglass motorboats, abandonment of speech,
    Japanese floral arrangements, spillways,

summer on the Dalmatian coast,
the shooting of Anton Webern.

FONTAINEBLEAU: FEEDING THE CARP

After a formal tour of the park and gardens
we visit the palace itself, traipse through the state
apartments. We look down at the pools and gardens
through upper-story windows, sprinklers playing
on the grass. And, coming down, we go out
to the carp pond, look down through the murky water
and see whole schools of them, fat and hungry,
looking up at us. A small child teases them
with cigarette butts and candy wrappers. In dismay
we offer them what we have—bits of cheese,
crusts of bread, even half an apple. They eat it all.
And, when we have nothing more to give, we walk back
through the gardens to our car and drive out into the forest.
For a while we play king and court among the trees,
climbing and walking, or riding to the horns. And then,
cold and hungry, we stumble into Barbizon, village of artists
and models, and starving, but still in love,
we hang ourselves in a garret.

FIRST LOVE

The street before your house
was all dug up. They were laying
pipes or pulling them out again.
The sidewalk stones were propped up
against trees. Long trenches lined
the street. I had to walk the plank
to reach your watery embrace.

PRAIRIE JUNCTION

The land is an anvil
and everything here is hammered flat.
At the corner is a filling station.
You can pull off the road
if you want to.

Two roads cross each other here at hard
right angles. One runs exactly east and west,
the other north and south. Each day the sun
follows the one, from one horizon to the other.
Twice a year it stands directly over it,
beating down.

The filling station is low and squat
with a flat roof. It was built ten years ago
of concrete blocks and then whitewashed.
Before that there was nothing here.

If you stand in the middle of the intersection
and face north by east, you will see a lake
about ten miles off. It is an oblong smear of blue
set in a slight depression in the plain.
Summers it is shrouded in haze and waves of rising heat.
Migrating birds pause there on the way north
or south, but no one lives there. No fishing is allowed.

If you pull off at the station for gas,
a young man with a shock of yellow hair will
eventually come out to help you. His name is Everett Jones,
although you wouldn't know that. Everett works from eight
in the morning until ten at night, and lives with his wife
and three children in a town about thirty miles from here.
He plays his radio all day long.

No trucks go through anymore. But geese still fly overhead
and east-west traffic yields to that going
north and south for no particular reason.

WILD HORSES

White curly hair,
although he was not old.
But he thought
of his youth as gone.
Of himself as silent
and peculiar.
                Women had always liked him,
and yet he had always hated the photographs
where they'd stand at his side, smiling
toward the camera, holding his arm.

There was one he had liked, the one
with the queer face, the one who was always
talking about horses. She was the one
who had said there was nothing
as beautiful as a herd of wild horses
running loose in a high mountain valley.
What had become of her? he wondered.

MODUS VIVENDI

Living is simple, no big thing.
Food is everywhere. I only have
to take it. I eat garbage and old
rubber tires too worn to be recapped.
Radiators rusting in junkyards
start my juices flowing.

As to shelter, I never have to worry.
The top of my head keeps the rain off my brain,
and I sleep inside my skin.
A manhole is a mansion to me
when its cover's fitted snugly into place.

And love? Lice love me, and flies
and worms. Sometimes stray dogs take up
with me. And sometimes I with them.
I have no lack of friends, my friend,
and life is good to me.

NEIGHBORLY

You always went insane at Easter.
The lawn of your rented church,
always neatly trimmed,
the choir singing like well-fed beagles.
Your English doctor probably
found it difficult to imagine
why you said he had only his "solitude"
to keep him warm, when all he wanted
was that evil might be weakened by
the right hope, properly expressed.

INTIMATE VOICES

This,
on the water
by the bent trees,
sky the color of steel—

their boat slipping through the reeds,
birds flying up,
a gentle splashing of oars

sound of a voice whispering,
"I'll murder you.
I'll kill you."

      ◊ ◊

Stars mixed with smoke,
smell of burning meat. Dogs barking,
children crying in the night.

Whenever I walk out I see you there.
Doing what? I say. Doing what?
The hill stands above you like an older brother.

Moonrise. And still I have not finished with you.
The sky is flooded with moonlight. And still
we have not spoken our last words.

LITANY

I know my obligations.
I must burn the dead leaves when they fall to the ground.
If the tree is sick, I must cut it down.
I must put it into the fire, let its spirit escape
to the sky.

When a stone cries out in loneliness,
I cannot ignore it, but must go to it and comfort it.
The polished pebbles of the stream-bed
also have their claim on me. Should they
cry out in the middle of the night, I must
go to them, take off my shoes and enter the water.
My feet must caress them.

My eyes are obliged to take all things in,
like a landlord with an infinity
of rooms. Nothing may be turned away.

I must speak as I can, with words
verging on silence.

II

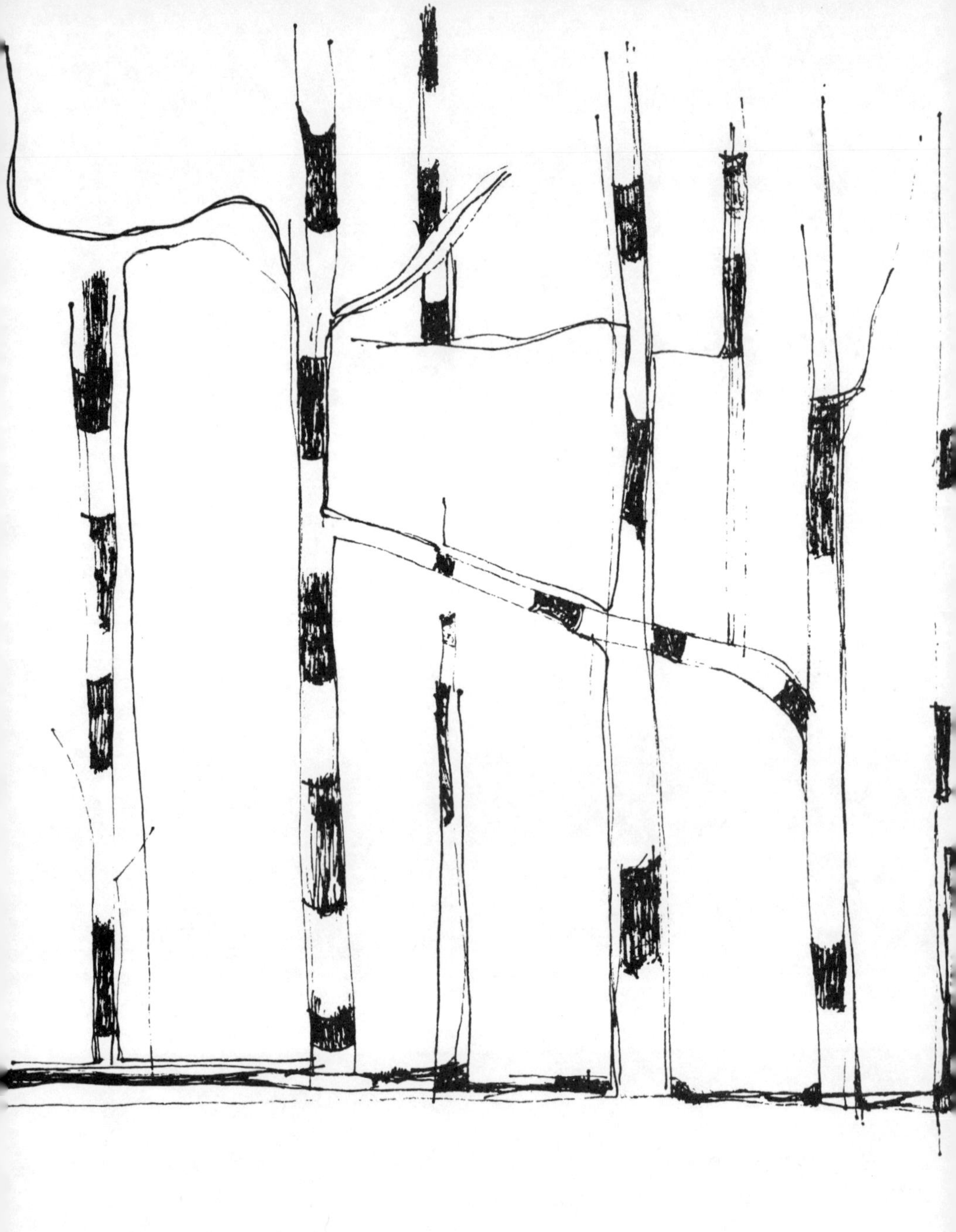

BARN

This is where the animals live,
in all their filthy brutishness.
In the early morning, long before sunrise,
I go down to watch them, to listen to them.
They seldom know I am there, but they
shuffle and stamp fitfully. Seven pigs,
twelve cows, and a horse. We have no need
for a horse, and still he lives here.
The cattle snort, and long columns of steam
erupt from their noses. The pigs make me sick
with their high squealing. Mice live here too,
and sometimes cats and birds. Chickens wander
in and out, but they have a house of their own.
I hate them all, the dirty, noisy things.
I'd kill them if I could.

MOIRA

A name shrieked out by the wind
on these moonless winter nights,
shouted down a hundred chimneys
in one small town, whistled past the edges
of loose windows and the world.
Moira—name of two small girls in this town.
One lies in her bed, staring in terror.
Who screams out after her, night after night?
she wonders. Who rattles the window
and shakes the door?
The other lies peaceful, uncaring,
behind the church. If the wind seeks her now,
he will not find her. Let him look for another.
In a town as large as this one
there might be another Moira living.

STAMPING

Late at night in my room
I like to practice the stamping dance.
When all is quiet and I'm sure the old man
downstairs is sleeping, I put on my heavy
winter boots and practice the stamping dance.
I stamp with my left foot, I stamp with my right.
Just over the bed where he sleeps.
I give him a left and a left and a right foot again.
Practicing the stamping dance, I stamp him
awake, right over his head.
I stamp and I stamp, until I hear his foot
—his cough and shuffle—on the stair.
He knocks timidly at my door, but I shout,
"Get away from here, old man" and wait
for him to fall asleep again.

OIL

I took a can of oil
and went all around the house oiling things.
Upstairs and down. I oiled the creaky steps,
the groaning floorboards—waxed these too.
I oiled the squeaking doors
and stubborn windows.
In every part of the house I found something to oil,
something that had once made noise
and now no longer did.
I listened to the sleek and shiny silence
of my house. No more nights of worry,
I thought, of funny little noises.
But then I thought of someone breaking in
and sneaking up on me—and now,
and now I wouldn't hear him coming till too late.

LIGHTS

Somebody doesn't like light.
He wrote on a wall that the whole town
should be dark after dark. When the streetlights go on,
he throws rocks at them until they break.
And if people show lights in their windows he smashes
their windows until they go out. The whole
town is afraid of him. He must be someone crazy.
It goes on like that for weeks and weeks
and nobody knows who it is, or what we ought to do
about it. Somebody smashes some windows,
and then an old man walking with a flashlight
is hit on the head with it and nearly dies.
But when somebody is caught it turns out to be a beggar
that everyone thought was blind. The lights, he said,
were so bright he couldn't see the stars.

SNOW

The temperature was dropping.
My heart—that jolly puppy—
was thumping its tail on the floor.
I bandaged myself up and walked out.
What had been a gray, solemn rain now became
rain mixed with snow, and then a light wind sprang
up and blew away the rain. Only the snow remained,
great white puffs of it, lowered on invisible
wires. Fluffs of cotton clung to my lashes,
got in the way of my eyes. I blew them away.
Whiteness was stretching itself out upon the ground.
The forest, far off across the fields, had a white screen
suspended before it. And the playfulness of it seemed
to infect us all. We put on the white of a hospital
where every illness was its own cure.

MOUNTAIN

When I think of this mountain
I mainly think of the tremendous
weight it must have. I think of mass—of *mass*!
The mountain moves heavily in its own way.
Its ridges are studded with huge, half-exposed boulders,
some perhaps ready to fall. Yet these are mere flakes
compared to the dense dark mass below, those shelves and columns
and slabs of subterranean rock. This mountain keeps
most of itself to itself—underground and deep.
And yet on its slopes and in its narrow valleys
it tolerates air and light, sunshine and shadow.
Clattering goats on high rocky ledges. Plunge of a stream
into forest, where voices cry out in surprise.
Beneath it all, the mountain—silent and sober. And
beneath the mountain, the dark and massive earth.

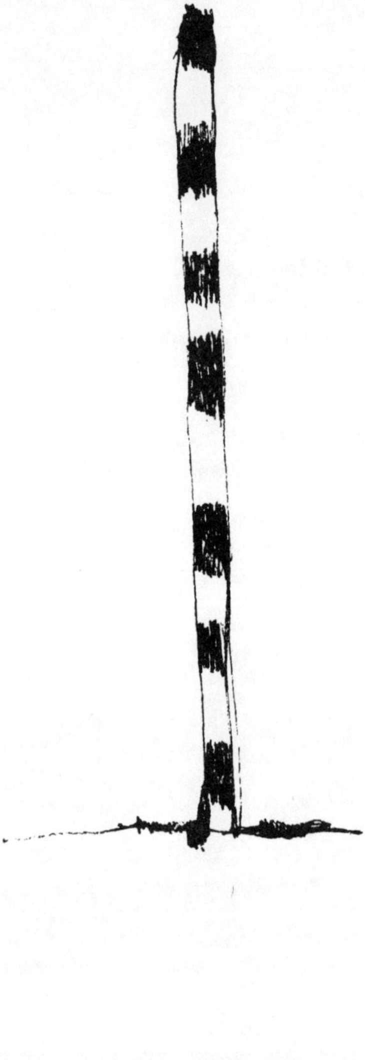

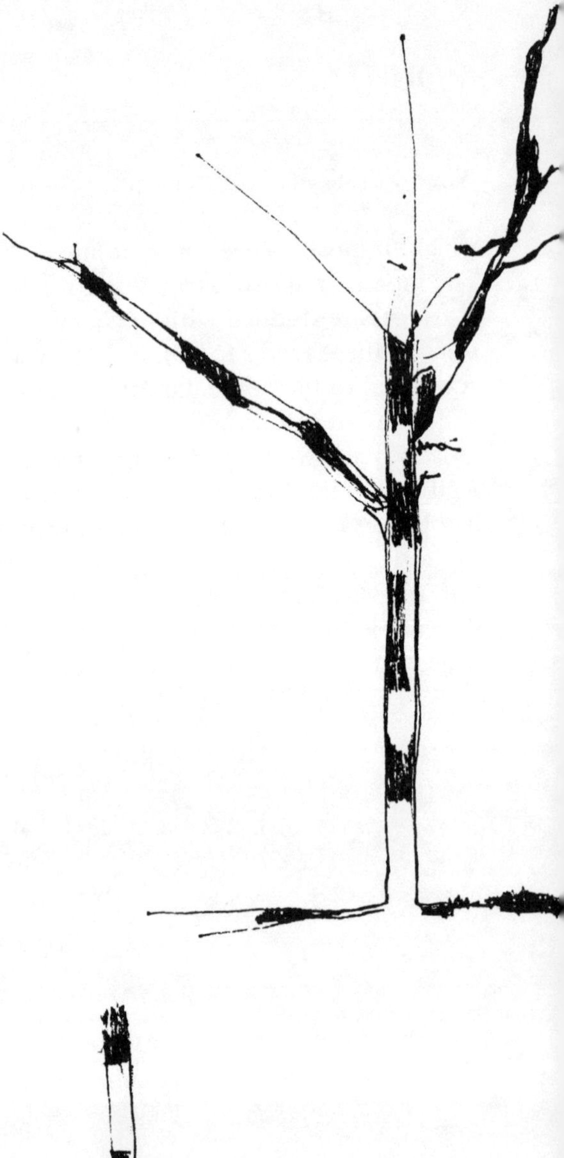

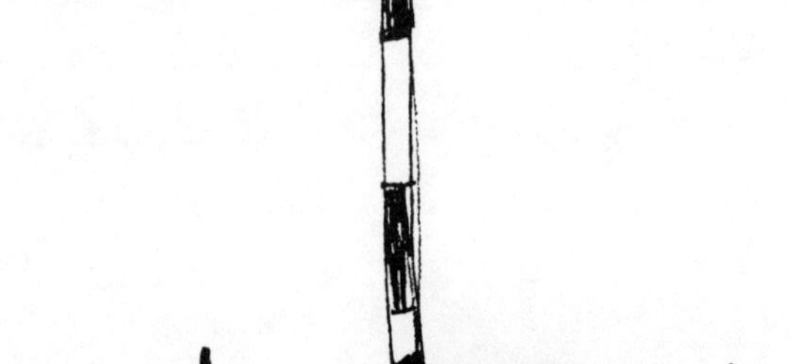

III

A BAD DAY

This was going to be my day.
But my alarmclock didn't go off
and I woke up very late.
I dressed in a hurry, but still
had to skip breakfast. I left
home without kissing the missus.
I slipped on some ice and broke
an ankle. The pain was something
awful. The taxi that was taking me
to the hospital blew a front
tire and spun into a lamp-post. The
driver was instantly killed, and I
had a broken arm and leg to go
with my broken ankle. An ambulance
came and took me to the hospital,
where everything was properly
set, and I was strung up in bed
like a puppet. At two o'clock
in the afternoon, a careless smoker
started a fire in the maternity
ward. Most of us patients were fully
evacuated, but a dozen or so babies
were killed or otherwise damaged.
Twenty-five other patients died,
some of whom were dying anyway. Ten
doctors and nurses were injured or
killed, and three firemen died of smoke
breathing. Police units were trans-
ferring us to another hospital when word
came that a series of explosions set
off by terrorists had wounded or killed hun-
dreds of people in the city. The
hospitals were jammed. I found myself
stretched out on the hardwood floor
of a high school gymnasium. The mis-
sile attack came without warning,
not even a blip on the radar screen.
The school was 90% destroyed, and most

of my fellow sufferers were 100% dead.
With my one good arm I managed to claw
my way out into the street, dragging
my useless legs behind me. To my
amazement, I found that this high school
was only a block from where I lived.
There was no one around, so, very painfully,
I inched my way home. No sign of the missus
there. The house was a shambles,
but the second floor was pretty much
intact, although somewhat lower.
Part of it drooped into the cellar.
My room was a mess. I hadn't had time
to straighten up. So, screw it, I said,
and crawled back into bed—which,
of course, I never should have left.

BEGINNING AGAIN

This was you—complete and nothing missing.
You were official, and the art of illusion
was well developed in you. You knew the difficulties
that strangers passing through were likely
to encounter. You were willing to run the risk
of asking unlikely questions.

If the train was late, you would be the first
to learn about it. Others sat near you,
gently prodding. In your stocking feet you would glide
toward the footlights and resume the song you'd been singing,
although you continually murder it. Somehow the image
of Grant's Tomb presented itself, and nobody
knew what to do or if anything ought to be done.

You had such beautiful hands. I wanted to carve them
in wood. If I could give you a present, it would be
respectable parents and five pretty girls
for sisters. At least that would be a beginning.

WALKING YOU HOME

Listening to Brahms,
I unzip my fly and rub myself up against
the lush impotence of the music.
It is as though nothing had ever happened
to change my mind about you.
The cat yowls and then yawns without missing
a beat. From the sky it appears
that small clumps of houses are festooned
with square necklaces of sidewalk.

Arranging to meet you for dinner
is part of my afternoon's pleasure. And later,
behind the infirmary, you are there,
still wearing your white nylons and your little
white cap. Somebody's puppy is leashed to a fireplug.
Even in such a town as this, there are park benches
on which no one is ever seen to sit.

After the movie, walking you home, I urge
you into the darkened playground. We swing on the swings,
hanging our heads back to look at the stars
upside-down. I get off to push you up higher.
Your bluejeans swim up from the darkness
and then away again. And then you're gone. The swing
comes clattering down. I try to coax you back. An owl hoots
and a car goes by. Never enough time to really talk.

DEPARTURES

As the evening here broke my bones
somewhere or other a coal-burning train
with a full head of steam
was chuffing off into a distance
continually receding.

OSTINATO

Our constant
companions
were a low murmur
and a pulsing
throb.

Their cabled
reflections
were a low murmur
and a pulsing
throb.

Your cancelled
affections
were a low murmur
and a pulsing
throb.

NIGHTS ON RAINY LAKE

Here is where I'd come to die.
Somewhere under the lake-edge pines,
I'd sit down, prop my back against
a tree trunk. Staring out across the water,
I'd barely make out the opposite shore
through darkness and shreds of fog.

Another night I'd build a small fire,
brew one last cup of coffee in a small pot.
Sitting back, I'd be conscious of my shadow,
above and behind me, playing in the trees.
As fire dwindles, the forest would move in closer.
In exquisite agony, we'd lie down in the dark together.

The last night, I'd go down to the shore,
climb into my canoe and paddle out onto the water.
The pines at the shoreline would vanish. Darkness ahead,
darkness behind. No moon, no stars. Dark water underneath.
Paddle on my knees, in the streaming silence, I'd sit there
barely breathing, waiting for the coming of the light.

DECEMBER MORNING

Besides Barbie and the cat
and the houseplants,
the first living things

I saw this morning
were two blue tits outside
the window in the appletree.

Barbie's gone to Nürnberg
for the day, and I'm left
behind to finish grading

papers for a course I'm teaching.
It's a cold morning. Sunshine
streams through the windows.

Tasha, the cat, sits
on the back of a chair in the living
room, watching the birds in the tree.

The roads are clear, but
the ground is covered with snow.
Blue sky everywhere,

and steep-roofed Bavarian houses.
Beyond the appletree and above
the roof of the second house

down the street, I can see
the bulbous tower of the church.
Its clock says exactly 10:30.

REFUSALS

You make yourself clear.
Your words issue forth
and come near me, moving
briskly in the cool air.
I wrestle them to the ground.

We stretch ourselves out
on the grass that is bluing
with evening. Somewhere
between us is an understanding.
But also an element of risk.

Stars extend their nightly
invitations. They beckon
through a universe
of remarkable transparency.
I issue my nightly refusal.

ETUDES

This is a piece I play
using the black keys only.
On the sidewalk across
the street, someone has collapsed.
No one rushes up in concern.
Why should they? Why should they?
Nobody's business but his own.

◊

Here is the song of the bomber
with clusters of notes
struck by my fist.
It is named after a smouldering
village, which none of us
knew the name of, even then.
My hand is bashing away at the keys.

◊

Less than ever
do I understand you. A trill
in the bass, third and fourth fingers.
I don't even know where
you come from.
The trill broadens to a tremolo.
I stare at you, wide-eyed in amazement.

◊

Here my left hand crosses
my right hand to pick out several
tones at the very top of my range.
I think of it as swallows,
darting, looping high against
a darkening sky. Or bats
swooping out of the attic at nightfall.

◊

Chords. Great majestic chords
moving out across
a landscape, like a column
of tanks. When broken,
there is a rippling effect,
a movement like that of water
moving swiftly over abandoned bones.

EROSION

Hello? The moon is high
in the sky. I wish that, as words
fade, you'd find the idea
right there in the landscape.

These others were trained
by me and my brother. Everyone
is wearing our specialty now —
sovereign mutations.

Going on kept both of us busy,
but this evening we sit among our
portable distortions. You could
say this is hard, to say this

is hard. It lets us jump gaps
in every direction, harmless snakes
winding in the shadows. But what if
a man could never relinquish,

if the light in his eyes never died.
Each effort insists on a natural-
ness of execution, a simpli-
city of expression. By midnight

the moon will have set. The moon
has never thought about you,
or considered your circumstances.
That room, so barren of ideas.

How ferociously . . . staying alive.
A woman's shoulder near my own.
What kind of garden in her mouth?

DAWNING

She is asleep,
one leg over the other.
Her mind slides through
a multitude of minds.
Another way, another
day is opening
at the morning.

MY LIFE IN THE REVOLUTION

I sit for hours
on a hillside
overlooking a river in Germany.
I see small birds
flying from tree
to tree.
Green things push
up among the dead
leaves on the forest floor,
and I watch,
I listen.

PRESSURE POINTS

I'm on the anvil,
and the hammer is coming down.

Everything in me pushes outward
against the boundaries of my body.

Earth presses up from below,
and the sky is bearing down.

You surround me, and everything about you
weighs heavily upon all my surfaces.

I am the hammer,
the head of a nail rushes up to meet me.

DOWN THE ROAD

Orion high ahead, and I'm leaning
over my steering wheel looking up,
on my way home after class.
Off to my left a wedge of moon
rises blearily through a cloudbank.

Sometimes I get tired of all this stuff.
Going off to work and coming back
again, sunsets moving north and south
and north again, the slow and steady
drift of seasons, shifting sky.

If you had it all to do over, someone asked
me the other day—if you had it all
to do over, would you do it again,
would you marry Barbie again? Would you?
If I had it all to do over. Well, would I?

Sometimes I'd like to keep going, keep
right on moving out of sight. If I were the moon,
there'd be months when I'd feel like trying out
another planet for a while. Well, sometimes I'd like
to keep going, down the road and out of sight.

NIGHTRIDE

Moon came out from behind
a hill. Didn't talk to
me much like it used to.
Moon was a waning gibbous,
hung like a ripe peach
over a small farmtown
and then moved on.

I was moving too. Down
below, me and my car, we
moved this way and that
over dark country roads,
winding around in the dark,
except for moon.

Moon played cat and mouse,
first one place and then
another, first ahead and
then behind, then off
to one side. Moon never
stands still. Neither do I.

CONVERGING LINES

Or three roads, say, coming together in a forest,
where no one has passed for several days,
                                        where the wetness
of the forest floor might allow one to pass unnoticed
although damp earth and pine-needles clung to his boots.

Or three persons, unknown to each other, converging
on a point in the pine-woods where three roads intersect,
but where no vehicles have passed for many years,
where fallen or cut trees have blocked the roads and never
been removed.

Someone moving along such a road would have to swing his legs
up and over the barrier that blocked it. His feet would touch the road
lightly, a fraction of a second before he threw his full weight
upon them.
                    In the moment of relative silence, his weight still poised
on the road-blocking tree, he would hear footsteps,
                                                  or perhaps
due to the wetness of the forest floor, the dampness of the road,
he would not hear footsteps. Or perhaps he would.

The three of them meeting in the forest. They would meet
in surprise, not knowing each other. They would touch
and say words to each other.
                                And then they'd walk on,
each taking the road of another.

NEARING THE MOON

Face facts. The moon is not the moon.
The moon is a lump of rock and sand and interplanetary debris.
But the moon is not that either. The moon
is a bump on the forehead of a blindman,
who, having tripped and fallen in an alley,
curses his blindness. Now we begin to approach it.

A WINTER'S SUN

I dream away in the cold light. The afternoon makes
its inscription upon the vast expanse of snow and ice.

At a place where most of the snow has been blown away
I brush away more with my hand until I get down to

the frozen grass, still green under all that whiteness.
And when I have cleared a place that is long and wide enough

I lie down there, on the stiff blades of grass. I lie
on my back, looking up at the sky through the black

naked branches of a tree. I dream away in the cold light.
The winter sun makes virtually no effort to warm me.

FAULT

It was only the first mistake,
a massive outcropping of rock
the weight of which was beyond our comprehension.
Strange that in such a sparse country
the birds should be so heavy.

WAITING ROOM

Fell from a high window
in love with a turtle soup and
never left her side, although
circumstances provoked hard feelings.

BRAIN DAMAGE

Mother is fine. She's warm
and brave and immobile. She rests
comfortably in her room. Of all of us,
she is the one who can most be
counted on, even in her present
condition. We all admire her.
Mother's fine. She doesn't want to see you.

Dr. Nevins stands above her,
honing his razor on a leather strap, one
end of which is attached to his belt.
She is trussed up on her bed. Her head
is already lathered. Millicent gasps
as the doctor begins to shave that lovely
hair without a hint of dullness or gray.

She's always enjoyed Dr. Nevins. He plays
a game of bridge which Mother always described
as "elegant." And now Henry Nevins is cutting
through her skull with a small circular saw,
no more than an inch across. It's plugged
into the socket just below the Watteau.
Millicent can't watch and leaves the room.

Mother smiles through it all, but if Henry
detects so much as a wince, quick adjustments
are made in the needles. Mother and Henry were
lovers once. Millicent doesn't know. But I know,
and you know. That was long ago. We were very young.
We were both disappointing to her, but you were worse.
She never learned to live with some of her disappointments.

Henry Nevins is inside her brain now. There are clamps
and bits of gauze and cotton and blood. No pain. Even
without the needles, the brain feels no physical pain. He's
done now. He's finished undoing the damage you've done.
The bowl of skull is replaced. The scalp is stitched into
place, and Mother's tidied up. So you can come home again.
Come on home now. Mother is fine. She won't even know you.

STUNT

Nothing much harder
than falling off a horse.
By grace of whatever—
no broken neck.

Ranging west,
driving across salt flats after dark.
High peaks—behind and to the north—
shrouded in darkness and tattered cloud.

Headlights pop up on the horizon,
steadily bear down upon you for half an hour,
maybe more—whoosh by—red taillights
jiggle in the mirror, half an hour more.

Nothing fades. It stretches and breaks.
The trick is to survive the snap-back.

DISAPPEARING INTO THE NIGHT

A rasp, a word.
The spell of rainwords.
A slick skin with the cat's fur
over it. Daphne often reminded
him of his obligations.

The hour strikes
and now it is eleven again.
The second time today.

Collecting figurines, their car
sped by on two wheels.
Small and plastic saints,
dolls with red lips.

His eyes followed the curvature of the earth.
His hand was on her knee.
Among the stars shining down on them
were several no longer existing.

Land of the minums.
Living among them.

BÊTE NOIRE

As far back as memory takes me,
my black darling, you are there.
In the shadows of my childhood
you wait to jump out at me.
After everyone has gone to bed
you wait for me in the dark kitchen.
Or in the bathroom. Or under my bed.
Sometimes you don't bother to hide.
I lie on my back and see you
hovering near the ceiling.
You pushed my teddy bear out the window.
From twenty floors up, I watched it fall
into the black hole. You taught me to live,
my dark darling, live in dim light
without that kind of loving. The one thing I loved,
plunging forever into darkness and rain.

AT MIDNIGHT

No one said, "Where are you going?"
The stranger remained where he was.
Midnight. The church bells rang the hour.
Another day—cycle of twenty-four hours—
was over. The cars moved away,
down the dark, narrow street.
The cattle moved heavily in the fields.
The silver fountain ceased to play.

EAGLE COVE

I could see you walking on the beach
far below me. You walked mincingly as though
the stones beneath your feet were sharp and jagged.
Putting the glasses to my eyes, I could see
that your feet were bleeding. Your eyes
were full of tears. Not once did you look up & see me.

Birds—white gulls—were screeching.
Time and again they sailed up on the sea-wind
only to plummet once more to the sea,
the tall spire-like rocks along the shore.

The distance between us lengthened. I walked away
from the edge of the cliff. Above one hill
an eagle hung motionless in flight.
Small animals in the brush below lived
in fear of a glance, died at full pitch
in a falling rush of feathers.

TRACK SOUTH

I was smothered, light-headed,
moving south with that free, subtle company.
The road to this place is slow
and unaccommodating. Running south.
Everything shivering.

Not lack of air, but their perfect
confidence oppressed me.
Two men succeed in raising the memory
of shelter, of painlessness.
One spoke of spasms and thundering stones.

I couldn't see it. Running south
in the dark, as though the never-ending road
were not fraught with peril. Three died.
The driver buried them. Their graves
were piled with massive rocks, survivors' gestures.

The gracious speakers gathered around
a fire. Our line of march had taken us
through a long, wide valley. The road
passed through lava-flows in weather
that reeked of the south now. The hot, stinking south.

PAVILIONS

Three wide yellow sheets hung before the sun,
their tops fastened to a line passing overhead,
bottoms staked to the ground.
From where I was sitting I could see
all three of them billowing before me,
bellying out with great gusts of air.

Later, a sullen music. I could hear the slow bullets
enter the water. Down at the edge of the sea.
The sun had set long before. Now they were lighting
the ocean with batteries of searchlights.
They were shooting the dolphins there.

My mouth was at her cunt, nipping and nuzzling.
My face was slippery with her juices, and my tongue
darted in and out of her. My hands stretched out,
slid up along her hips and over her soft stomach
to her breasts. I could see her head lolling
back on a pillow. She moaned and cried.

Her body was a holy temple to me now.
The street where I lived was deserted, there was
no one in sight. Knocking at doors aroused no one.
I reached my own house only to find I had locked myself
out. I shifted around so that my penis was only a few
inches from her face. She didn't need to be forced.

By now the beach had been lit by floodlights.
It was a bizarre sight. The searchlights playing
on the water. Small boats were now coming in, trailing
the bodies of dead dolphins behind them, depositing them
at the beach, and then going back for more.

δ δ

It was the sudden involvements that bothered me
the most, the urgent sense that situations beyond
my control could enmesh my feelings to such an extent

that I could never entirely disengage myself.
Touch, for me, was contaminated by my belief that
each contact with the other left some residue of myself
embedded beneath her nails or flaking off into empty air.

Specialists delighted in regaling us with facts and statistics
purporting to deal with ourselves. Each bit of emotion
could be graphed, or circumscribed by calculated limits.
Each line of action, real or potential, accurately charted,
projected through infinity.

◊ ◊

But when as children we had hung our tents
in the backyard, draping sheets and blankets
over clotheslines, we would then crawl inside
to play doctor or explorer in the diminished light.
And running my hands over her cool legs I would feel
her hand lightly upon myself and guiding me,
guiding me toward the emptiness at her center.

The room in which I was imprisoned was taller
than it was long or wide. A single window stood
high on the western wall. To look out I had to grasp
the bars and lift myself several inches above the floor.
Beyond the broad, level ground, which two days out of seven
served as a marketplace, stood a fantastically rich pavilion.

It would always happen that in the middle of the night
someone would come upstairs to the door of our room
and stand listening just outside. If we made any sort
of sound, the door would open a few inches and a voice
would say, "Go to sleep now. Go to sleep." Otherwise
we'd just hear footsteps going down the stairs
and the light at the floor would go out.

◊ ◊

For some reason, a decorative air vent had been cut
in the ceiling. During the middle hours of the day
a brilliant arabesque of sunlight appeared near the base
of one wall of my room, moved slowly across the floor,
and vanished halfway up the other.

There was salt in the air and the pavilion was continually
buffeted by a strong sea wind. Though not deprived of water
I was constantly thirsty. I had the strange sense of being near
the sea and at the same time hundreds of miles inland,
surrounded only by drifting sand or barren reaches
of rock and sun-baked earth.

On marketdays, crowds of people passed before my window,
and in the late afternoon their shadows paraded across my floor.
Her pavilion, fluttering like a huge, yellow butterfly,
presided over the scene. The sun set just behind it.
And later, single stars from dismantled constellations
would pass above me, impossible to name. And hearing
her voice come across to me, over the nearly deserted market,
I'd forget the stars and, once again, haul myself up to the window.

IV
IMPROVISATIONS

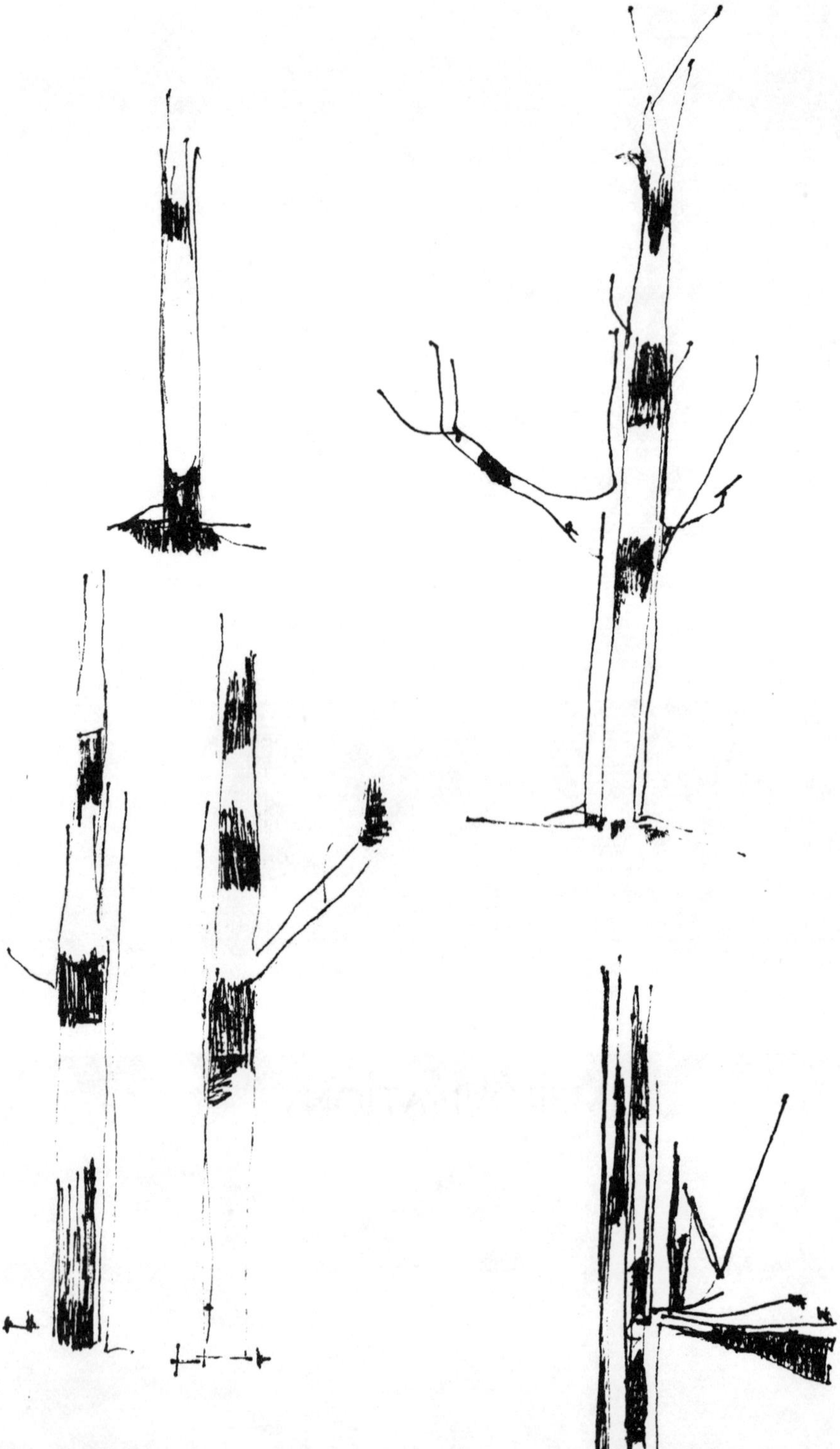

The trouble with America is
the trouble with all of us is
each and every one of us, the trouble
I tend to remember only the good things
but I cannot forget all the rest—
the imperviousness of the average man
to whatever seems to bother him the most
or what he is most reluctant to forget
and allow our troubles to slide from our shoulders
or else it would be simple enough to solve, wouldn't it?

At Dodona—
voice of a god in the rustling of oak leaves,
the ring of the whip against brass

    & now as the wind drops off and dies
    a lavender sky towers in the west

          there are no voices,
    two young boys dance to a wisp of flute

They tell the most outrageous lies.
The bus has gone off without us.

I lie down in the middle of the road.
Looking to one side, I see you approaching from afar.
You and your retinue ride slowly and with great dignity.
Behind you a cloud of dust rises into the sky.
I am naked, and as you grow nearer
I begin to masturbate.
I can now hear the sound of your voices.
The tromping of horses and creaking of leather increases.
I grow more and more excited. I can see your face.
Snippets of conversation reach my ears.
You are very close to me now, closer than
ever before. The wind whips your banners.
You ride right over me.

Utrecht, 1287.
O, there was screaming and mad dancing.
It started in town but soon moved to the bank of the river
and then (as they pressed us) to the bridge across the river.
We danced and we danced and we danced. They swarmed upon
us, beat those of us near the end of the bridge, but
could not move us. We danced and we danced. Others joined us
and we danced on. Shouts and singing filled the air.
Then there were so many of us wildly dancing
that the bridge, with a mighty roar, collapsed beneath us.
We swam for our lives and those who could not swim were drowned.
If the bridge had not broken we would be dancing yet.

If you would only listen to me I could
transform you. You are a stick
and I an ant scurrying along your entire length.
I could be a knife stripping the bark from you
in smooth, steady motions. If you were a stick
I could be a dog, carrying you in my mouth,
running in long leaps and bounds,
returning you to my master.

Blue sky above, much like
that of Norway. The forest is laid out
with narrow, dirt roads—miles of them,
branching off in various directions,
some leading off into thick stands of spruce
or dense groves of oak and pine and larch.
Here the ground is littered with broken branches,
pine cones and bits of dead leaves and needles.
But elsewhere there are evenly stacked piles
of lumber—entire trees cut into exact
lengths, the segments varying only in
diameter, as though with patience
and effort you could stack them end to end
and make a tree again.

But it was another day
and whatever daylight had to say
could not be taken seriously. Holding everything
at arm's length seemed to do it.

By day there is a shine on things. The water
has a skin of light. And we have
no sense of anything in hiding there.

I will take you up into the attic.
I have the power right here in my hand.
You shall see what has until now been denied you.
My hand will lift aside the curtain of an attic window
and we shall look out over the rooftops. Between the branches
we'll see the river flowing southward in the distance.

V

EDGE OF THE FOREST

Just now, after an argument with Barbie,
I climbed on my bicycle and rode over to the forest.
I rode through the little German town where we live,
and out across the fields. No one was working.
It was evening, just after supper, and the churchbell
was ringing. Looking back toward the town, its cluster
of steep-roofed houses and barns, I could see the bulbous,
onion-shaped dome of the church rising above
the neighboring roofs.

I had taken a wandering route through the fields,
following one narrow dirt track and then another. Finally,
I turned onto one which skirted the forest. After riding
along for a bit, I stopped, got off, and kicked down
the bike stand. Leaving the bike in the road,
I walked to the edge of the forest.

Suddenly, it had become very still. The bike was an old one,
and on bumpy roads it squeaked and rattled loudly. It was
the absence of this that I took, at first, for silence.
But then, as though blossoming, the forest burst into sound.
There were chirps, buzzes, whirrs, rasps—the sounds
of birds and insects I could name in neither English nor German.
It was an elaborate mosaic of sound, and all I could single
out was the distant rapping of a woodpecker.

Soon enough though, the distant sounds of humans threaded
their ways among these. A kilometer away, cars sped by
on the road from Burgoberbach to Rauenzell. I heard
a helicopter in the distance. And soon there was a German farmer,
his tractor pulling a wagon, coming out into the fields
for a half hour's work before dark. From where I stood,
the sun was halfway down into the trees. The sky was bright and clear.

The forest is typical of our part of Germany—tall firs
or spruce, and sometimes a stand of oak, very little undergrowth.
Essentially tree farms, these are forests that men walk in.
This one has known human life, it is said, for ten thousand years.

I confronted the forest. The fields and the town were behind me.
The sun was becoming more orange as it set. I was still
sharply tuned to the weaving sounds around me.

I thought of our life together, our life in Germany,
Barbie's and mine. And, facing the forest, I felt that
the forest was simple—the trees, the birds, the insects—
a simple mindless thing. Simple in its beauty and simple
in its brutality. In the fields behind me, German farmers had,
for centuries, coaxed food from the earth. And gone into
the forest to hunt. But when the churchbell rings, they,
with prayerbook in hand, walk to a church built by men.
Our life together, Barbie's and mine, is beautiful
and, in its way, brutal. In our farmland and forest, we graze
and kill for love. And love is what we eat.

Turning back toward the fields, I saw some leaves against
the sky. They were full of tiny holes, countless tiny holes
eaten by insects in the new leaves. In the distance,
the houses and barns, their roofs steeply pitched to shed
the snows of winter, crowded around the church.

I started toward my bike and then stopped. Two young deer,
less than thirty meters away, had come out of the forest to nibble
at the new May grass. I tried to make no sound. One lifted
its head and peered at me. It craned its neck for a moment and then,
though I hadn't moved, decided I couldn't be trusted. Turning,
it ran in high leaps through the field and back into the forest.
The other stood staring a moment longer and then plunged
into the safety of the trees. They were gone.

For a few minutes I could hear them barking in the forest.
Half-bark, half-yawp, a sound I'd heard before from deer I'd
startled in the woods. But strangely the barking continued
close at hand. Then farther on, beyond where the first two deer
had been, what I had taken to be a stump raised its ears
and let out an answering yawp of its own. Now this one
had heard me, since I was on my bike and moving. It paused at the edge
of the forest, looked once more at me, and then it disappeared.

THE INCALCULABLE PERFECTION OF HEAVEN

The first time I visited that house
lace curtains gently swayed to and fro in the windows.
Front and back, the lawns were neatly cut and trimmed.
Rectangular flowerbeds were crowded with marigolds, nasturtiums,
and other flowers, the names of which I have long forgotten.
The driveway, consisting of two concrete tracks, ran alongside
the house to a garage at the back. The garage had the old, hinged doors
that folded back to either side, not the modern type
that slide up overhead on metal runners. Along one wall, or half of it,
there was a wooden workbench cluttered with tools, odd-shaped scraps
of wood, jars and cans full of nails and screws, and countless
curled shavings of wood amid the inevitable sawdust. License plates
from previous years were nailed on the rear wall. In the corners
and at irregular intervals along the walls leaned shovels, rakes,
hoes, pieces of pipe of various lengths, storm windows, and screens,
in the process of being washed. The floor had accumulated the usual
mixture of dirt, oil drippings and bits of last year's leaves,
overlaid by flattened cardboard boxes. The coiled garden hose
hung near the door on a constellation of nails hammered into the wall.

PARADISE ROAD

Down the blue
they all move out
of here. But all
of them were breathing.
The gypsy girl—her earrings,
coughing, everything.

It's snowing. We try
to keep warm by jumping.
Along the road is a high
wall with jagged glass set in the top.
We're all alone in the world.
The snow is still coming down.

We tried to believe their stories.
They smiled and cajoled us, but we
were not taken in. And then
we were on the platform
of a train station, and they
had come to say goodbye.

My grandfather—with suspenders
and his big gold watch—was there.
He smiled and waved. So did they all.
The gypsy girl coughed. And then they left.
The train stood still. It was the world that moved
away. The world moved away without us.

SALT SPRAY

At the edge of the sea
salt spray freezes in my beard.
The wind comes at me out of nowhere.
My hands are aging.
Wrinkles do not bounce back.
They are digging in
as peasants do,
preparing for the long winter.

THE SEA AND SINBAD'S SHIP

Far from home,
sailing a sea neither friendly
nor hostile to us. Plying our trade
in the much-maligned towns of that coast.
Their women were known as small-breasted
and cheerless. Then why were we so happy?

At sea by day, the sun held us under
its burning-glass. Distant islands
fumed in watery glaze. Hot breezes
pressed us slowly up along the coast.
Our ecstasy: taut line between sky & sea.

Nights in port were a drunken splendor.
Deserted by the bitchy women, we drank
and sang and puked the night away.
The lives of sea-going men, we sang.

Nights at sea: sea singing sweetly
under our keel, stars slipping by overhead,
spray on our faces, the night sea-wind.
Ship on the sea, sea under ship,
cupped in the hands of earth and starry night.
Our brooding silence was a wail of joy.

A LITTLE STREAM

I ran along the bank of a little stream.
I ran and I ran and I ran and I ran.
I sat at its edge. My feet dangled
in the water. I lay on my stomach,
writing my name on the surface of the water.
But in fact I have forgotten my name.
The stream runs along without me.
It runs and it runs and it runs.
Through meadow and forest, by boulder
and tree. Beside smoking abandoned farms
and small, dirty villages. It runs
red with blood, and the sound of screams
is lost in its idiot burble.

SIX CROSSINGS

The first time we crossed it
by foot. It was a slatey gray,
but dusty and wrinkled like
old elephant skin. Rosalind
wanted to turn back, but the
rest of us were against that.

Our second trip was completely
uneventful. Absolutely nothing
happened to break the monotony.
What can I say about a boring,
uneventful trip during which
absolutely nothing happened?

On the third crossing we used
two-seat hovercraft for the first
time. We lost the Martinsons
that way: crashed, burned. For
the others though, the broader
perspectives were encouraging.

A general malaise pervaded
the next excursion. Perhaps
the loss of the Martinsons
accounted for some of it. But
even after the most thorough
analysis—unanswered questions.

The fifth crossing: our only
unqualified success. The signs
were good from the very first
day. Wheeled vehicles humming
along at a steady pace. What joy!
What elation! What ecstasy!

The last one, of course, could
not live up to the one which
preceded it. But Rosalind insisted.
"For the Martinsons," she said.
Tomorrow we reach home again.
Tonight is our last night out.

NOVA

If it were up to me,
I would let you see everything.
You could tour the universe,
witness the end and the beginning.
You could feel what it's like
to be sucked into a black hole
and spit forth on the other side.
You could explode like a nova,
feel yourself hurtling out from a center,
bright and fast, at incredible speeds,
in the darkness of space, scattering light.

LYRIC SUITE

1.

We sat on the porch, enjoying what was left
of the morning. Across the road a clump of salt cedar
lifted its fluff into the clear, dry air.
There were three of us, plus a dog. He and she
were speaking in low tones of a mutual concern.
Occasionally they would turn to me—not to consult me,
but as though the rule of hospitality required that I
be included, even where I could not reasonably enter.
At length, they felt free to ignore me, and their voices
droned on in the rising heat. Their dog bluntly refused
to accept me. Every muscle in his body was tense.
He stared at me and sometimes bared his teeth.

2.

It was their life in the country I envied.
Their house sat at the crest of a low hill,
and their property sloped down and away in all directions.
Here I would take long, solitary walks, rambling among
the stubborn plants of the desert, picking my way
among the rocks and boulders of dry stream beds.
Day by day, the strict economy of the desert
claimed more and more of my attention—how these
scrawny sticks and misshapen lumps of cactus
made do in a landscape of lack and adversity,
how the animals—mangy coyotes, half-wild dogs, rabbits,
snakes, lizards, turtles—clung to the margin of life.

3.

Evenings we'd listen to music. Usually chamber music,
a small group of strings. A Haydn quartet, say,
the brilliant first violin lording it over the others.
Or Beethoven. What more perfect, more honest,
more intimate conversation than those last quartets!

In the following silence they would go to bed
and I would walk out to the edge of the desert,
where the only sounds were rasps and moans and howls,
unimportant successes and failures of small and smaller things.
And, feeling a kind of singing, I'd know that the same death
claimed Beethoven, Coyote and me. And returning then
to the house of my host I'd be greeted by furious barking.

WINTER JOURNEY

Listen! This morning
I got up early. It was
dark out and raining.

I shaved and dressed
without waking Barbie,
didn't even turn on

the lights in the bedroom.
Our dirty, orange VW camper
started reluctantly, or so

it seemed to me, also
a reluctant early riser.
It was six-thirty.

At the corner, I picked
up a GI, some kind of
Chicano or Puerto Rican,

who said he'd been waiting
there for an hour. I took
him down the hill into Ansbach

and deposited him at another
corner where he stood
a better chance of getting

a ride to where he was going.
Ansbach was dark and cold
in the early morning rain.

The cobbled streets were shiny,
reflecting the lights—red,
yellow, white—of the few

cars and trucks already on the move.
I was heading north towards
Schweinfurt, an hour and a half

away, over winding German roads.
The radio was tuned to some
early morning dreck on Bavaria 2,

which was better than
nothing, as I hurtled past
the silent, German farms.

There were lights on in
some of the barns though,
and I could imagine

the thick, Bavarian
farmers moving among
the cows and pigs.

The asphalt paving
turned to cobble
at the edge of Lehrberg

and I rattled through town
and out the other end.
Nothing much moving there.

The next towns—Gräfenbuch
and Markt Bergel—were
farm towns. Lights in the barns.

I sped through Ottenhofen
without slowing down,
crossed the railroad tracks

and then shot past the turn-off
to Illesheim—muddy old
army post, teaching every day.

It was still dark. The last time
I'd made the trip, two weeks
before, it had been lightening

by now. The trees of the Buchheim
cemetery could be seen clearly
against the brightening sky.

Today there was nothing.
I barely saw the cemetery
as I flew by. I'd been promising

myself to stop and take some
photographs there. Now I made
the same promise again.

It was just a small, country
cemetery with a stone wall
around it, two leafless trees

at opposite corners.
Uffenheim was next.
Another farm and market

town, but this one large
enough to be a county
seat. Uffenheim was

a hilly town, and, as I drove
up and down its dark, hilly
streets, there were young

kids on the sidewalks,
trudging to school. No,
"trudging" is not the word.

German kids don't trudge to
school, they walk briskly
with their heads down against

the wind, their books in
colorful packs strapped
to their shoulders. They

seem to know where they are
going and why, even on Saturday
mornings before dawn. In rain.

One sharp descent had led down
into Markt Bergel, and leaving
Uffenheim I was headed

toward another, which began
at a small church on my left
and dropped steeply down to

Ochsenfurt on the left bank
of the Main. Between Uffenheim
and the church, a distance of

eighteen or nineteen kilometers,
the sky had begun to gray.
Farm wagons were now slowing me

down from time to time.
Cars were more numerous too.
At Ochsenfurt the highway

crossed the Main and ran
along between the river
and the hillside vineyards.

The radio ("Bayern Zwei") was now
playing classical music on its
early concert—chamber music

by Donizetti and Rossini
this morning. I thought about
the class I was going to teach,

a session on the utopian motif
in American history. Twenty
GI's within a seventy-mile

radius of Schweinfurt had
signed up. At eight o'clock
I tune to AFN and catch five

minutes of the news in English.
I drove through Sommerhausen
and Eibelstadt, two Main Valley

towns with gate-towers
at either end. It is getting
lighter quickly now, and by

the time I reach the autobahn
it is almost full daylight.
On the autobahn there is

a constant flow of traffic.
This stretch runs from
Frankfurt to Nürnberg, but

I turn north toward Kassel
at the Biebelried intersection.
Schweinfurt is less than

half an hour away now.
The cars and trucks on the
autobahn throw up clouds

of wetness in their wakes,
each one seems to be moving
in a constant spray of water.

The autobahn moves more
imperiously over the north
Bavaria hills than did

the local road, which curved
sharply with the hills and slowed
down for the towns and hamlets.

The farms—quite large ones here—
are becoming visible in early morning
mist. Sloping down and away

from the highway, they look
like huge, curving slabs
of mud. The autobahn, two

wide strips of concrete pavement,
passes alternately through
farmland and forest.

It is occasionally paralleled
by muddy farm roads, wagon
tracks through the rain-sodden

fields. Two centuries running
parallel to each other on
a gray, December morning.

I never see Schweinfurt.
Conn Barracks is on the outskirts,
and my green USA plates

get me on base without so much
as a pause at the gate.
It was eight-thirty now,

and I drove directly to the snack bar,
where, starving, I had a good
American breakfast—two eggs

over easy, sausage, home-fries,
toast and coffee—served to me
by a stocky German frau

with a bit of broken English.
Two or three GI's were eating
at nearby tables, the jukebox

was blaring. Class began at nine.
Some four hours later I was on my
way home, back to Ansbach. Fifteen

of the twenty had shown up.
There'd been an hour and a half
of half-hearted discussion

of the American dream and what
went wrong and how it seemed to
start going wrong right at the start,

Jefferson's words about freedom
and the slaves he never quite
got around to setting free.

There was a short break and then
they sat down to write their mid-
term essays, which I gathered up

two hours later and stuffed
into my briefcase. Army bases
are all alike. I went back

to the snack bar, had the same
lunch I might have had in Ansbach,
heard the same stuff on the jukebox,

climbed into the car again and drove off.
There's the same boredom, the same
sullenness about them. So, leaving

Conn, I was back in Germany again,
whipping along the autobahn,
traffic much heavier now. The trucks

I passed were throwing up great sheets
of water behind them, and as I went
round them I'd been momentarily

blinded as the windshield wipers
failed to keep up with the deluge
of water. I thought of Barbie,

getting up late for a change,
sleeping perhaps until mid-morning,
then rising and taking

a shower. They're all alike,
the army bases, like they're punched
out on a printing press, decals

slapped onto the surface of Germany,
one just like another. At the Biebelried
intersection I turned west toward

Frankfurt, but I got off where
I had gotten on. Full daylight now,
a cloudy, rainy afternoon.

The clouds are an uneven gray,
with brighter patches here and there.
The road surface shines, and I feel

like I am driving on the sky.
I wait at the gate to Sommerhausen
while a car comes through the other way.

At Ochsenfurt I cross the river
and climb the hill. For just a moment
I think about stopping at the church

at the top. It's just a small, country
church, but it looks like it might
be interesting. I might take

a picture of it someday.
On a hill I pass a slow tractor
pulling a wagon full of sugar beets

and suddenly there is another car
right in front of me, coming out
of the rain. We both swerve

the same way. There's a loud
noise and the brightest flash
I've ever seen. Then black.

But in some part of me
I am still driving south. I dip
and wind through Uffenheim.

The kids are home from school.
The cemetery at Buchheim lies
in daylight now, its intricate

trees stretched against the sky.
But I don't stop. I didn't bring
the camera. I pass the turn-off

to Illesheim, drive through
Markt Bergel and climb the hill.
Three towns more and I'm back

to Ansbach. I park out in front
and go in. Barbie's up now.
I say, "Hi!" She's sitting at the desk

with her back to me. "Hi," she says,
without turning around. I tiptoe
up behind her, kiss the back of her neck.

She turns around then, smiling,
but when she doesn't see me says,
"Where did you go? Where are you?"

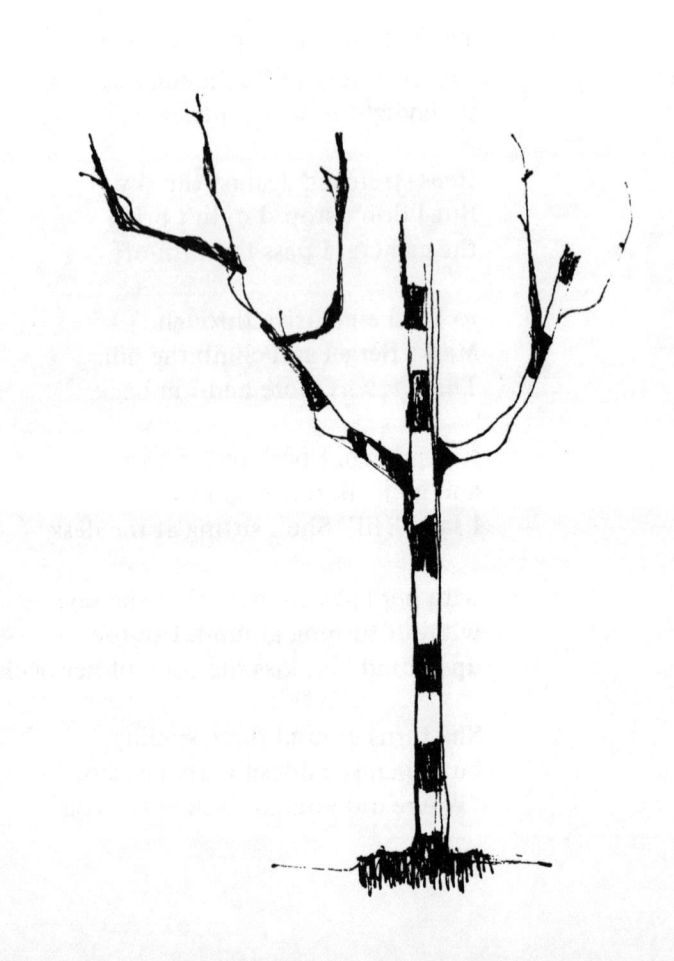